Gospel
BASICS

Gospel

BASICS

Victor R. Scott

Passionate Publishing
Cordele, Georgia

Victor R. Scott
Gospel Basics: Seeing the Goodness of the Good News

© 2011 Victor R. Scott
2nd Edition

Passionate Publishing
Cordele, Georgia
jeremiahspassion@gmail.com

Formerly Printed as *What is the Gospel?*

ISBN-13: 978-1456399283
ISBN-10: 1456399284

This book is dedicated to

Miranda
my beautiful wife, for she has freed me
to do the work that God
has given me to do

and

The youth group of
Pittman Park
United Methodist Church
Statesboro, Georgia
who allowed me to teach them
God's word (2006-2009).

Acknowledgements

There are several people that I would like to thank. First, my wife Miranda for proof reading the initial text. I appreciate the thoughts and suggestions offered by my friend, Pastor Rodney Bradford. Many of his insights helped to sharpen my thoughts and clarify key concepts and ideas. I want to thank Kyle Constable, for reading the full text and providing a needed clarification.

I would like to thank the staff of Snowbird Wilderness Outfitters who provided a caring and Gospel saturated environment where even this "professional Christian" was confronted with the Good News of Jesus.

I am thankful for all of the input and support. I bear all the responsibility for any deficiencies in this text. My prayer is that it be used for the Glory of God, to help promote genuine faith and the clear declaration of the best news I have ever heard.

READ THIS FIRST!

One of the hardest decisions about writing a book, any book I would imagine, is finding a way to get into the subject. And even though this is like other books, the subject of this book, in my opinion, is not like any other book. I am not saying that I will do a better job than others that have talked about the Gospel of Jesus Christ. My desire in this book is to *not* assume that the reader understands what the Gospel is. As I have worked as a "professional Christian" over the last decade, I have grown in my conviction that this has been the mistake, that has brought the church, in her modern expression, to the place where it no longer displays the power the Bible says should be present or is fulfilling the purpose for which it was established.

Why do I say this? I say it because every denomination is in decline in America. What is causing this? If this trend does not change, it is growing dangerously close to becoming nothing more than a shell of what it is supposed to be. I cannot say that the state of affairs in the church is *only* because the Gospel is misunderstood. This would be an over simplification. What I will say is that at the heart, or said another way, the root cause of the decline that is seen in the church is because the radical, life-changing and ultimate nature of the Gospel has not been upheld.

How can I justify such a claim, you might ask. Allow me to pose one simple question. Before you read the question I would like to provide some instructions about what to do. After reading the question write down your response in the space provided. Answer as honestly and as accurately as you are able and then continue on reading. Please do not proceed into the book without finishing this part.

What is the Gospel?

_____

_____

_____

_____

Now that you have answered the question how do you feel? Was that easier or harder than you thought? Why or why not? How comfortable would you feel in sharing this definition with someone who is a Christian? How about someone who was not a believer? How confident are you in what this means for your life?

These and so many more questions run through my mind as I have thought about why the church does not see the results that seemed to punctuate the centuries of church history. I refuse to believe that the manifestation of the Spirit's convicting power was reserved to the centuries past. I refuse to believe that God has given up hope on this era of human history. I refuse to believe that the Good News is no longer good, for all who shall hear it and receive it.

If we claim to be Christians and we are unable to answer the first question that leads to the very life that we are claiming, there is a very **BIG** problem. And when you discover that you, as a "professional Christian," are unable to answer the question there is a really BIG problem. As I have been awakened to this in my own life I have had growing sadness about the fact that the reason that the church is in the state that it is in is because it starts, not with the institutions, but with each individual who fails to know and live and declare the truth that leads to eternal life.

I am well aware that there is an "American" bias to these comments. And to a large degree I am talking to the church in America. But there have been throughout our history great movements of God that have changed that character and complexion of our moral and religious landscape. I have grown tired of the defeatist attitude and language that seems to be pervading the church. Why are we trying to maintain what we have instead of taking ground from the enemy of God? Why do we feel that protection is a better path to achieving the will of God than invasion of the kingdom of this world? The language of warfare is all over the Bible, but it is a warfare based not on the physical world, but the spiritual. The battle that we wage is not with our hands or with weapons, but on our knees before an almighty God.

In June of 2011, I was reminded of the fact that the warning found in Amos 8 has not yet come. The prophet tells us the following:

> 11 Behold, the days are coming, declares the Lord God, when I will send a famine on the land not a famine of bread, nor a thirst for water, but of hearing the words of the Lord.
> 12 They shall wander from sea to sea, and from north to east; they shall run to and fro, to seek the word of the Lord, but they shall not find it. (Amos 8:11-12)

There are two things that stand out from this text. First, there is a day coming when the "word of the Lord" will not be found in the world. That appears to be clear. But, there is another truth that is also there and just as true that we, as the people of God should never forget. That time has not yet come. There is not a famine in the land, not yet. That means that every-thing that the bible says about the Gospel is still just as true today as it was 2000 years ago. If this is not reason for hope and a call to action I don't know what is. I will never be the same after the events that I have witnessed in that last year. I will never go back to being an "average" Christian. I will never again fail to speak the truth of God's grace out of fear.

The rest of this book will unpack some of the most important facets of the Gospel. This is not intended to be comprehensive, but my attempt of providing an outline of some of the key concepts and truths, as I understand them, that make the Gospel what it is, and ultimately what makes the Gospel Good News to hear.

TABLE OF CONTENTS

Chapter 16:

Conclusion:

Appendix

PREFACE

This book came into being as the result of a winter camp/ski trip while I was serving as Youth Director in Statesboro, Georgia. Over the course of those three days, we were challenged over and over with the Gospel—the message of Jesus. Near the end of our time there, I was becoming frustrated and began to wonder why I had this tension inside of me. Then, in a moment that must be described as illumination, I realized it was the Gospel presentation that was frustrating me. The youth pastor of a church frustrated with the Gospel!

It was as if for the first time I had recognized an assumption that I had made. I believed that I had outgrown the Gospel. It sounds ridiculous now, but at the time it made sense. During the final day I approached the camp director and shared with him what God had shown me and what I had learned.

The Gospel is not just the point of entry into the family and kingdom of God. The Gospel *is* the Christian life. The full expression of the Christian faith is found in living and proclaiming the Gospel of Jesus Christ.

I returned home and decided to investigate again the truth of the Gospel. Over the course of four months, I sketched out the depth and breadth of the Gospel from my study in our church's newsletter. The articles were not an exhaustive attempt of presenting the Gospel. My desire then was in whetting the appetites of my church family, as it is now of you the reader.

What is written on these pages is just the beginning. Allow the following pages to challenge your thinking and reignite your passion in and love for the Gospel.

Victor Scott
Cordele, Georgia
2011

WHAT IS THE GOSPEL?

Over the course of my journey of faith I have come to understand that the Gospel is more than "Jesus loves you. Accept Him into your heart and you won't go to Hell." Having such a simplistic view of the Gospel is to diminish everything God did in sending Jesus to redeem the world. I agree that salvation from hell is a wonderful thing. But, there is one thought that rises to the top: is this all that we have to be thankful for? Is release from judgment the end of Christ's work of redemption? I believe that the Gospel is much richer than this.

The Christian's freedom from hell is an important and definite benefit of our salvation. But to reduce the totality of what Christ did for the believer to this is a violation of God's word and Christ's work. And to the degree that this view is held or used to describe the Gospel there is work to be done to correct the trivialization of the Gospel. This is the mission of the church: To faithfully present and proclaim the Gospel. Anything short of this objective will give those who are listening to a distorted picture of what God did *in and through* Jesus.

The Gospel is a simple message, but it requires those of us who have believed it to understand the full and complete implications of God saving us through Christ. This means that whenever something is left out of the message it distorts the whole. As followers of Jesus, we have to get this right and we cannot edit the Gospel to make it "easier" to understand.

Once we have the basics of the Gospel in our minds we must take the time to internalize and apply everything the Gospel demands. This book is an attempt to remind us that there are many streams of biblical thought that have to be understood to truly understand the full implications *and* applications of the Gospel. My desire is to give as full and complete a picture of what God gave in the Good News of Jesus Christ.

The Gospel is primarily a message about God's reconciliation and adoption of sinners into His family. It is against the backdrop of these actions that God speaks through Jesus to us. My goal is to highlight the fullness of God's love toward us. As we look at the whole Gospel we will see that God was not careless. God did not forget anything at all.

I will reiterate the Gospel here so that you can see what *must* be included. I say "must" in the sense that these are the essential truths of the Gospel. Everything mentioned here does not need to be said all at once when the Gospel is shared, but it should be understood by the person sharing it. The following chapters will unpack the Gospel message as it is summarized below. My heart's desire is for you to see how deep and wide the message of Jesus truly is. This is my understanding of what the Gospel is:

> God is Holy and good. No man, woman or child is able to live up to God's perfection. Because of God's nature, in order for humanity and God to have their relationship restored, something must be done. God is also just and must therefore punish sin, which means missing the mark of God's standard. No one can do anything worthy of God's forgiveness because it would not be equal to the offense. We simply do not have enough moral virtue to repay God.

> The only way that sin could be dealt with and God could remain just was for God to send Jesus. Jesus is not tainted by a sin nature, the inclination to sin, because He is God. Jesus can stand as our representative before God and bear the full and complete burden of God's righteous wrath because He is like us—

human in every way (except for sin). This is the mystery of the Incarnation. Because of Jesus' sacrifice on the cross, He paid for our debt of sin and gave to us His righteousness, allowing God to extend grace (undeserved favor) to us sinners.

As a result, all who agree with God that their sin was deserving of Jesus' life, death and resurrection and believe that this is enough to restore relationship with God will be born-again. This reality will be confirmed by the Holy Spirit, who is God, and will give each new follower of Jesus a new nature. This new nature will desire to leave sin behind and to turn to God for strength, direction and the courage to obey the truth of the Bible.

This is the Gospel! I have spent years trying to understand how this works. What I have come to realize is that the "how it works" question is not as important as this question: How do I live this truth? The Gospel is designed to glorify God, bring life to repentant sinners, renew worldly minds, and restore ultimate purpose to all who believe in Jesus. All of this comes within a love-relationship with our Heavenly Father.

If we look at our lives and they have not been changed we must wonder if we have heard the Gospel at all! Have we felt the love of God in our lives? When we think about the Gospel, is it still Good News to us? Paul's words to the Romans are the driving force for this study:

What is the Gospel?

> For I am not ashamed of the gospel, **_for it is
> the power of God for salvation_** to everyone
> who believes... (Romans 1:16, emphasis added)

My hope and prayer is that the promised power of Christ would be seen in my life and in the lives of those that hear the Gospel, not just for the first time, but every time. The Gospel is the source from which we receive what we need to continue fighting the good fight of faith (1 Timothy 6:12). Let's now look together at this Good News that Jesus came to proclaim (Luke 4:16-21).

THE JOY OF THE GOSPEL

We had just gotten back from our ski trip and as I thought more about my youth group's time in North Carolina I kept going back to one theme that was shared with us — the Gospel of Jesus Christ is not just *a* reason for Christians to have joy in their lives. The Gospel is ***THE*** reason to have joy.

One great danger in talking about the joy found in and because of the Gospel is that we think that what God did is about us. This would be a misunderstanding of what it means to have the joy of the Gospel. Peter helps us to see that there are new realities now that we have been saved (1 Peter 1:3ff). We have an inheritance that is guarded by

God himself in heaven, that our trials are not meant to destroy us but to grant us assurance of what we have believed. We could look to Paul's declaration that we have been granted new life and a new nature (2 Corinthians 5:17). These reasons for joy are not because of anything we have done, but are fully dependant upon God's work in Jesus.

The Gospel is the power of God unto salvation to all who believe (Romans 1:16). The Gospel is what God has prescribed as the doorway to new life in Jesus. There is no other way for anyone to receive salvation (Acts 4:12; John 14:6).

The Gospel speaks to the joy of salvation from the jaws of death and hell. What greater story could there be? We no longer fear what is to come. Paul told the church in Thessalonica that we do not mourn like the world does. We have something wonderful to anticipate which is the joy of being in the presence of Jesus forever (1 Thessalonians 4:13-18, 1 Peter 1:3).

The Gospel is a message that leads to a new relationship not only with God, but with ourselves and those we encounter. We will relate to God and to those around us in a new way. This new relationship is marked by our love for one another (1 John 1:7, 4:19-21).

The Gospel cuts a new path we have to walk. This means we will have to make choices that will separate, or rather distinguish us from those around us. Christians should look different from the world around them (Matthew 7:13-14).

The Joy of the Gospel

29

The Gospel has power, but it also provides purpose. We have been given a new ministry to fulfill. Paul called it the ministry of reconciliation (which means to have the relationship restored). We are given the privilege of participating in God's proclamation of the Good News (2 Corinthians 5:16-21).

The Gospel is a message of hope, but it sends us on a mission of peace. We should recognize that the Prince of Peace (Isaiah 9:6) has come to give us a peace that surpasses our human abilities to understand (Philippians 4:7).

Yes, the Gospel is Good News! This is just the beginning of all that God has to teach us in and through the message of Jesus. I thank God for reminding me of the ***Joy of the Gospel***.

The *Joy of the Gospel* comes when all that God intended to happen because of the message of Jesus becomes a part of who I am and how I live as a child of God. When I think and breathe and desire to enjoy Jesus in everything, joy—true joy—will run in my heart and mind without stopping.

REJOICING IN THE GOSPEL

If the Gospel is good news, why don't more Christians live with excitement about the Gospel? I speak for myself (and to my shame), but there have been many times when I have grown tired of hearing the Gospel message. During the ski trip to North Carolina, I was reminded of the Joy of the Gospel and shared with you some of the reasons why lasting joy is found in the Gospel. But why doesn't this seem to last?

When a non-believer hears the Gospel of Jesus and the Holy Spirit uses that message to awaken their heart, that person is changed. The way the Bible describes this change is that we are "born again" (John

3:1-8). This is a miraculous and wonderful moment in a person's life. The Bible says that the angels of heaven throw a party when someone has been born again (Luke 15:10). If the angels are that excited about someone becoming a Christian, our excitement ought to be as much, if not more than theirs. When an unbeliever is accepted into the family of God, we have just witnessed a miracle. Awe and wonder and thankfulness are the appropriate responses to this event.

When we are born-again we have been given a gift of incredible worth. Salvation is a costly gift that was worth Jesus dying to get it for us and to us. We must grow to treasure the gift of salvation. It is not something that grows old or wears out. We have been brought into the family of God. Paul said it this way, "But now in Christ Jesus you who once were far off have been brought near by the blood of Christ" (Ephesians 2:13, cf. Ephesians 1:3-14). This is what it means to be adopted. This is what happens when we are born again.

I have been challenged to not only remember the Joy of the Gospel, but also to rejoice in the Gospel. What does it mean to rejoice? Webster's dictionary provides this definition: to feel joy or great delight. It is something that I am doing in response to what God has done. Another way of thinking of what it means to rejoice is that it is to re-joy? To remember what God has done and is continuing to do in and through us. Have you "re-joy-ed" today in the Gospel?

THE GLORY OF GOD

We have looked at the Gospel and have seen the reasons that we have joy in and through it. Now I would like to take a closer look at what the Gospel actually is. Over the next few chapters, we will journey together as we uncover the richness and depth of the Gospel. I want you to keep in mind that these are the basics and all of these should be kept in mind when thinking about the Gospel.

The first basic of the Gospel is that the entirety of the Gospel can be "book-ended" with the same thing – God Himself. To understand the Gospel we must see that salvation, and all that it promises, is grounded in the person and work of God (Ephesians 2:8). The Bible opens with "in the beginning God…" and it ends with God's return in Jesus Christ. The reason the Gospel is so important is because it is God's news to a fallen world.

The Apostle Paul wrote that "all have sinned and fallen short of the glory of God" (Romans 3:23). The idea here is not that if we keep trying we can get this right. Missing once has completely messed up our average. We will never be 100%. Never. We have fallen short and if God doesn't get involved we will never be able to measure up.

The idea of glory is a description of God's utter and unpolluted perfection. The Gospel begins with the impeccable beauty of God and it ends with the impregnable grace of God. When we begin to see who God is, we will have a better understanding of the problem that faces sinful men. The Gospel begins with God. If it begins anywhere else we risk missing the message God delivered in Jesus. It is God who saves so that no man could boast in themselves (Ephesians 2:9). If we ever lose sight of this reality we run the risk of destroying the only message of hope available to the world.

THE HOLINESS OF GOD

The Glory of God reminds us of God's complete perfection. This is an important concept to understand if we are going to make sense of the Gospel. But, God's glory is not the whole picture. God is also Holy. In the Bible these two words are not synonyms even though they are related. Holy means "to be separated from" and specifically to be separated from a desire or capacity to sin. In the last chapter, we saw that God's glory is related to his perfection. So, God is full of glory and is therefore Holy. Or, if we put it another way, we could say that God's nature is so perfect that he cannot tolerate sin and is incapable of sinning.

What this means is that because of God's perfection there is a gap—a very wide gap—between God and humanity. We cannot reach up to God and God will not reach down to us. Our sin is so bad that God has to destroy it in order for him to interact with us. But God does not make a distinction between the sin and sinner who commits it. If this sounds bad, it is (Romans 3:23). The Gospel is the way that God is able to bridge the gap. We will see this later. For now remember that sin has created a chasm between us and God.

If the Gospel is to be effective the devastating truth that the Gospel describes must be accepted as the actual state of affairs by the hearer. The separation between us and God is not a matter of miles, it is a matter of the heart. The human heart does not naturally bend toward God. If God does not first act upon us we will never turn toward him (Genesis 6:5; Jeremiah 17:9; Matthew 15:19). The bible never attempts to soften this truth for our convenience.

Within the Wesleyan theological tradition this activity of God is described as Prevenient Grace.* God extends His grace to us, calling us away from sin and sinfulness to follow after Him. The Gospel requires a proper understanding of God's holiness because that is God's standard. Anything less than holiness is sin (James 4:17). Until we see sin like God sees it we will give ourselves a break and will not take

* "Prevenient Grace" is understood as God's grace that comes into our lives before we have any knowledge of our need for God.

sin and its effects as seriously as we should. Look at how God puts it:

> "For I am the LORD your God. Consecrate yourselves therefore, and be holy, for I am holy" (Leviticus 11:44a).

This is the challenge of being a Christian. We must recognize and accept what the problem is before we will know what needs to be done to fix it. The problem is that God is holy and we are not!

THE BIRTH OF SIN

In this chapter I will be drawing a distinction between "Sin" as the condition of the heart, the reason Jesus was crucified, and "sins" as those things that we do as the byproduct of our nature.

Sin is one of the most difficult concepts to explain in the Christian faith. I make this statement carefully because all may not agree. We no longer seem to know what Sin is. Sometimes, I am amazed when people do not know what to say when I talk about Sin. The word "Sin" is considered a topic that should not be discussed in polite company. This may be part of the problem.

So, what is Sin? Where did it come from and why is it such a problem? There have been several attempts to define sin and even more theories on the origin of Sin. What I would like to do is to make the case that the origin of Sin is not a matter of time, nor a matter of when, nor is it a matter of who created or orchestrated Sin, but rather a matter of where.

Where is Sin born? Or in other words, what is the source–the root–of Sin? I believe when we get to the heart of the matter Sin comes from a twisted idea and the more that this idea is believed the worse off we will be.

Sin is an issue of the heart. Jesus said that it is out of the mouth that comes all kinds of evil because it comes from the heart (Matthew 15:17-19). James also said that "whoever knows the right thing to do and fails to do it, for him it is sin" (James 4:17).

The Prophet Isaiah gives us a picture of what is believed to have happened to Lucifer, the chief arch-angel of God, before he rebelled against God:

> 12How you are fallen from heaven, O Day Star, son of Dawn! How you are cut down to the ground, you who laid the nations low! 13You said in your heart, 'I will ascend to heaven; above the stars of God I will set my throne on high; I will sit on the mount of assembly in the far reaches of the north; 14I will ascend above the heights of the clouds; I will make myself like the Most High.' (Isaiah 14:12-14)

The Birth of Sin, I believe, is found in the perversion of free will. When we think that free will provides us with the ability to choose how we are going to live and that we can live in any way that we want, we are marching closer to Sin. When we make any attempt to remove God's authority from our lives, we are heading toward Sin.

In the end, this is the genesis of sin, our attempt to look within to find freedom and power rather than relying upon God. Without God's enabling Spirit we will not be able to do what pleases God.

> 12 Therefore, my beloved, as you have always obeyed, so now, not only as in my presence but much more in my absence, work out your own salvation with fear and trembling, 13 for it is God who works in you, both to will and to work for his good pleasure. (Philippians 2:12-13)

Paul encourages the Philippians to work out their salvation and in the next phrase he says that the only way that it will happen is for God to provide the motivation in the first place. As long as we hold to a distorted view of free will the tendency to rely upon ourselves and thereby continue to sin will continue.

Sin can be seen in the world every day. Sometimes we may not want to acknowledge it, but it is there. Sin is expressed in the world when we say in our hearts, sometimes in obvious ways and other times in more subtle ways, that God is no longer necessary for life. When we give ourselves the freedom to choose what to do or how to live without consulting with God we are near to Sin, and may very well be sinning.

THE BIRTH OF SINFUL MEN

King David tells us in Psalm 14 that the fool has said in their own heart, "there is no God." If Sin finds its birth in the perverted idea that God is not necessary, where do sinful men come from? They come from the practice of this thought. In the book of Genesis the enticement for Eve was not the fruit. The temptation was the possibility of being like God (Genesis 3:5). This was the trap, desiring what should only, and does only belong to God.

Every adult knows the bliss of child-like innocence. There are things that we just wish we didn't know. As we grow, we no longer have the luxury of remaining naive to the ways of the world. We can no longer keep thinking that the world around us isn't trying to distract us from being obedient to God's commands. The Devil will use any means at his disposal to make us vulnerable and to distance us from God (1 Peter 5:8).

The sinful tendencies of humanity are the result of its persistence to pursue what only God can comprehend. Why do you think that so many find the problem of evil the greatest "proof" for why God does not exist? Only God can make sense of it.

That is why when we sin we are standing in the wrong place. We are standing where only God belongs. God is sovereign. We should step down from His throne and trust that "for those who love God all things work together for good" (Romans 8:28). Even the things that are hard to understand.

THE REMEDY DELIVERED (PT. 1)

One of the most wonderful aspects of Christianity is that God is not far off. God is not so distant that He cannot be known. God is not so mysterious that He cannot be found. It is one of the greater wonders of the Christian faith that God has come down to earth and made His abode with humanity.

The doctrine of the Incarnation, that God became a man in the Person of Jesus, is relevant and essential to the Gospel because it speaks to the seriousness of the Sin and the graciousness of God. Only God could resolve and reconcile the broken relationship between humanity and God; and the broken relationship between humanity and itself. When we minimize the the significant role of God becoming like us, we undermine the message of the Gospel. John says it this way in his first letter,

> 2 By this you know the Spirit of God: every spirit that confesses that Jesus Christ has come in the flesh is from God, 3 and every spirit that does not confess Jesus is not from God... (1 John 4:2-3a)

The apostle John captures it succinctly when he says that, "the Word became flesh and dwelt among us" (John 1:14). God has literally pitched His tent in our midst and has condescended so that we may have access to Him.

Peter Lewis in his book, *The Glory of Christ*, makes this powerful statement about the miracle of Jesus being delivered through Mary's womb.

> "If this humanity is less than full and true, then He is inadequate as a mediator; incompetent as a sympathizer; and disqualified as a redeemer. If (save for sin) He is not all that we are in our uttermost humanity, then He cannot perfectly represent us either in His life or in His death. If He does not descend to us from God, then He cannot lift us up to God....it is in the Humanity of Jesus that we encounter the nearness of God" (pg. 142-143).

The Gospel message makes no sense if the Savior is not like the sinner. Only one who is like us can stand as an advocate, as a representative and plead for salvation on our behalf (1 John 2:1-2). And so we are confronted with the Incarnation and its importance to the Gospel message as we begin to see that Jesus had to become like us so that we could become like He is (1 John 3:2-3).

THE REMEDY DELIVERED (PT. 2)

During the Easter season, I am confronted with the same question. I find myself asking it during that time of the year, "Was there another way?" While it may be an interesting intellectual exercise the answer to this question is a resounding "No." The way of the cross is the way God has chosen to supply redemption to sinners.

When we go down this line of wondering if God could have or if God should have provided for salvation in another way we are calling God's wisdom into question. We must be careful of the reasons we pursue this kind of questioning. When God looked at the problem of sin, and considered what it would take to remedy the problem, the solution that God chose was the crucifixion of his Son. That is a drastic choice. But it has been made. We should be cautious in our second guessing God.

As one reads the Gospels, it becomes obvious Jesus understood that the culmination of His ministry would be death (Mark 8:31, 9:31; Matthew 16:21; Luke 18:31-34). Jesus was not caught off guard. Jesus was not surprised. Jesus knew that the reason for his life was so that he could die for the sins of the world. That was His mission.

However, there is something else that is woven into the fabric of the biblical narrative. The crucifixion of Jesus of Nazareth was not an afterthought as a response for Adam and Eve's sin. This would be a short-sighted understanding of Jesus ministry. The cross was the intention of God from before creation (1 Peter 1:18-21 [*see below*]; Acts 15:13-18; Ephesians 1:6b-10).

As Christian people we value Free Will and it can be difficult to resolve the tension that this discussion raises, but the Bible reminds us that we are responsible for our own response to the Gospel. We should not be afraid of God's freedom and right to reign over creation in whatever way God deems appropriate, even if we don't understand, and especially when we don't understand.

The remedy was delivered just as God had planned and determined. Glory to God! The following passages shows this in the Scripture.

The Remedy Delivered (Pt. 2)

22 Men of Israel, hear these words: Jesus of Nazareth, a man attested to you by God with mighty works and wonders and signs that God did through him in your midst, as you yourselves know— 23 this Jesus, delivered up according to the definite plan and foreknowledge of God, you crucified and killed by the hands of lawless men. (Acts 2:22-23)

18 knowing that you were ransomed from the futile ways inherited from your forefathers, not with perishable things such as silver or gold, 19 but with the precious blood of Christ, ... 20 He was foreknown before the foundation of the world but was made manifest in the last times for the sake of you 21 who through him are believers in God, who raised him from the dead and gave him glory, so that your faith and hope are in God. (1 Peter 1:18-21)

4 But when the fullness of time had come [the predetermined time had arrived], God sent forth his Son, 5 ... so that we might receive adoption as sons. (Galatians 4:4-5)

These passages give me reason to be thankful and grateful that my salvation was not something God was trying to figure out after he created the universe. God planned and executed the perfect plan to make sure that salvation was provided for sinners.

It is beyond the scope of this book to look at the interaction between free will and God's sovereign will. It will be sufficient to say here that the Bible teaches both. The way that each reader chooses to understand the relationship is for the reader to study and determine.

The cross of Jesus Christ was not an accident and it was not plan "B". The crucifixion was God's intended remedy from the beginning. When we understand that the cross is the only way for anyone to come to know and receive salvation through Christ, we will begin to move forward in our understanding of what God is trying to do in the world by the preaching of the Gospel.

COMMIT TO REPENTANCE

One of the aspects of the Gospel that is many times misunderstood and incorrectly described is repentance. Repentance is not merely feeling sorry for doing something that has offended God. Repentance is being contrite, it is seeing the hurtful and offensive nature of our sin against the holiness of God.

Repentance begins with Godly sorrow. This is the result of our not merely knowing we have offended God, but being completely disgusted with it. We just can't see ourselves continuing on in sin.

For the kind of sorrow God wants us to experience leads us away from sin and results in salvation. There's no regret for that kind of sorrow. But worldly sorrow, which lacks repentance, results in spiritual death. (2 Corinthians 7:10, NLT)

One of the biggest misconceptions is that repentance is a one time thing. We must commit ourselves to repentance. Repentance literally means the turning away from sin. But many times we mistakenly believe that our lives will require only one course correction.

Sin is always around us, working against us and tricking us into believing that we have arrived (Romans 7:10) and everything is alright. There is no arriving while we walk this earth. There is no "being alright." We are on a journey toward heaven and the path toward eternal life is paved with various opportunities to mess up.

We must be constantly moving toward God's presence (Psalm 105:4, Jeremiah 29:13). It is because of this striving that we must commit, whole-heartedly, to turning away from sin. Paul said, "For I do not understand my own actions. For I do not do what I want, but I do the very thing I hate" (Romans 7:15).

Paul was familiar with the Olympic games of his day and used an illustration from athletics to help the Corinthians understand that the life of faith should be run so that you win the prize (1 Corinthians 9:24, Philippians 3:14)—eternal fellowship with God. Repentance, I believe, is the means by which God adjusts our course in life so that we can run the race of faith well. Look at what Paul says,

Commit to Repentance

> Every athlete exercises self-control in all things. They do it to receive a perishable wreath, but we an imperishable. So I do not run aimlessly; I do not box as one beating the air. But I discipline my body and keep it under control, lest after preaching to others I myself should be disqualified. (1 Corinthians 9:25-27)

Paul desires to remain qualified in his faith and so should we; therefore, we must be constantly evaluating what we do in light of Scripture and God's character to finish the race that we have started. We have the added promise that God will not quit on us even when we feel like quitting on ourselves (Philippians 1:6). We should emulate Paul's example as we live the Gospel out in our lives.

The first time that we understand and acknowledge that we have sinned against God we repent. This is not the last time that we will need to repent. Our journey of faith is marked by growth and growing pains. At each of these points we may need to turn again toward God. Repentance is an ongoing process of changing our minds from what we think is right to what God says is right. Commit to repentance.

WHAT DOES IT MEAN TO BE BORN AGAIN?

This is the question that a man named Nicodemus asked one night when he came to see Jesus in a garden (John 3:1-15). Jesus had gone to pray and here comes a member of the Pharisees, a ruler in the Jewish community. Nicodemus wants to know what it is that Jesus is teaching and asking of those that choose to follow Him. Jesus, in answering the question, points to an unusual moment in the history of the Jewish people, an event that Nicodemus would have known and remembered because of his training.

For four-hundred years the Jews were slaves in Egypt. They called out to God and asked for Him to save them out of this terrible situation. God chooses Moses, a Hebrew who was raised by the Egyptians, as the one who is going to save them. God saves the entire nation, shows them where to go, gives them food, miraculously preserves their clothes so they do not wear out and yet the people keep looking back to Egypt as if the predictable life of slavery was to be preferred to the unpredictable life of faith in God. You can read the whole story in the book of Exodus (chapters 1-20). It is quite interesting. But Jesus is pointing to a specific instance during this journey toward the Promised Land.

The people became disillusioned with how God was doing what He did. Rather than continuing in faith, they made a foolish decision. They decided that they were going to complain rather than remember what God had done. Because of the nation of Israel's impatience, God sent "fiery serpents" among the people and as a result many died (Numbers 21:6). God instructed Moses to make a serpent of bronze and then to set it on a pole. If you can think of the symbol for the medical profession you have an idea of what this may have looked like.

God told Moses that anyone that looked upon the serpent would be healed. Nothing else is given. The faith of the individual would be confirmed by their trust in the instrument that God designated. Jesus is drawing a parallel between the events in the desert and the act of faith that leads to being saved, being "born again." Jesus was crucified by being nailed to a tree so that if I would look to him for salvation, God would fulfill His promise to save me.

Being born again is the act of looking upon Jesus, believing that the benefit and healing and salvation that God has promised will be transferred to us through the act of putting our trust in the instrument of the cross and in Jesus the Crucified.

Salvation is a leap, but it is not a leap over a cliff into the unknown. Salvation is a leap into the promises of God. The question that God forces us to answer is this, "Will we look to Jesus and receive the redemption that has already been offered?" (cf., Hebrews 10:1-12).

YOU ARE A NEW CREATION

As we have been looking at what the Gospel is we have not touched on one key question: What is the Gospel's ultimate purpose? This question has a two-fold response. First, The Gospel gives God the honor that He rightfully deserves because, second, sinners are recreated into new creations. Sinners are not just rehabilitated because they are bad people. To say this is to come far short of what God has told us is the problem. (We looked at this in chapter s 3 and 4). I heard Dr. Ravi Zacharias state that God did not send Jesus to make bad people good, but rather to make dead men live. There is a big difference between the two.

Those who say that the Gospel's purpose is for the salvation of the world diminish the revelation of God's character in the Gospel (Psalm 79:9, 1 John 2:12). Those who say that it is to appease the wrath of God make God out to be a petulant being (Nahum 1:1-15). God is sober in all his judgments. Therefore, we have to read the Bible and clearly decipher what it says to us regarding the Gospel's purpose.

Those who say that it is because of God's love and grace that the Gospel was given and continues to be offered fail to see that justice cannot be ignored on account of His patience (Romans 2:1-11, especially v. 4). God cannot and will not overlook sin forever. His holiness and glory forbids this from happening. Defending God's grace and love should never become the primary concern of the believer. When we do this we run the risk of looking at God's hand rather than at God's face. The former is to revel in God's benefits, while the latter is to be enthralled by God alone.

In light of these alternatives, I find Paul's declaration in 2 Corinthians 5:17 to be interesting and enlightening. He says, "Therefore, if anyone is in Christ, he is a new creation. The old has passed away; behold, the new has come." It speaks to a reality of what God desires for all of creation. God is looking to recreate sinners into a people that are able to know Him as He is. Only when we have been made to look like Jesus are we able to serve God and our neighbor adequately.

In Colossians 1:16 Paul tells us that "[Jesus] is the image of the invisible God, the firstborn of all creation". The idea here is that in Jesus we find that creation was to have an existence similar to that of Jesus Himself. Jesus is not the first creation, but is before creation. The word "firstborn" here speaks to his primacy over all things. He comes to us because God has sent Him (John 3:16, John 6:29, 1 John 4). The importance of this to the Gospel is that in Jesus we find the purpose of creation—it is for Jesus (Colossians 1:16).

But there is a problem; the creation has fallen because of Sin. The presence of the Gospel is God's remedy in and through Jesus to correct the wrong of sin. The only way for that remedy to take effect is for there to be a new creation, not only in the world (Revelation 21:1), but also in the inhabitants of the creation.

**The Gospel's ultimate purpose
is re-creation.**

A NEW JOURNEY

The salvation that the Gospels herald produces new life in us when we are born again. It fulfills the purpose of God in re-creating us into the creatures we should have been from the beginning . Finally it puts us on the road of a new journey. We are on a journey to a new land. We should never forget that this world is no longer intended to be our home.

The writer of Hebrews captures the beauty of this in telling us:

> "8 by faith Abraham obeyed when he was called to go out to a place that he was to receive as an inheritance. And he went out, not knowing

where he was going. ... 10 For he was looking forward to the city that has foundations, whose designer and builder is God" (Hebrews 11:8, 10).

By faith we believe and live and journey with God. We are not called to know the destination. All that God gives to us is the assurance that on this journey we will walk with Him through the trials and triumphs that life will hurl our way. Paul reminds us that "we know that for those who love God all things work together for good, for those who are called according to his purpose" (Romans 8:28).

Even Peter spoke of the transient nature of the people of God in this world (1 Peter 2:11). This world is not our home. The quicker we realize that our faith in Christ has altered our trajectory from eternal suffering to eternal joy the more we will prize and participate in the process of growing in our understanding and living the Gospel. God truly does love His children and we can be "sure of this, that he who began a good work in you will bring it to completion at the day of Jesus Christ" (Philippians 1:6). God is calling us to join Him. He still desires to walk with His people, if they would but come (Genesis 3:8).

SUBMIT YOURSELF UNTO THE LORD

Some time ago I had a thought about how God desires for us to relate to Him when we are confronted with the Gospel. Taking the time to think through these questions and others will help us to put into perspective what may be lacking in our faith, or what we are getting right. The line of thought that I followed revolved around two words—Submission and Surrender. While I believe that both are aspects of the Christian journey, the more I thought on it the more I leaned toward submission as the appropriate response to God and the Gospel.

God desires for His children to grow in faith and relationship with Him. This seems easy enough. This process is called sanctification (which I explain as "the process of becoming like Jesus"). So, we have to ask ourselves: why is sanctification important? It is important because it serves as an indicator of the progress we have made in our walk with God. Are we striving for God's will? Do we see the world through His eyes? When the world around us looks at us, who do they see? Do they see me, or do they see Jesus because I am a growing and changing person? If the answer is not Jesus we have to stop and rethink what difference the faith that we claim is having.

Submission and Surrender are both a part of this unfolding drama in that it reveals to God the inclination of our heart. What is the difference you may be asking? I would say it is an issue of choice. When I submit I am voluntarily and intentionally ceasing from pursuing my own program. I have decided to defer, to consent to the will of God and to let God determine what my goals, values and desires are supposed to be. In essence, I am conceding that what God thinks is more important, more accurate and more desirable to anything I may come up with.

Surrender, on the other hand, is different in that it implies the end of a valiant, yet fruitless attempt to win against the opponent. Surrender is being forced to back down under compulsion. It is waving the white flag because there is no other alternative. God does not want to crush those who hear the Gospel, but when we do not allow the truth of God's good

Submit Yourself Unto the Lord

news to change our minds and touch our hearts we will be on the wrong end of that exchange. Matthew records this exchange where Jesus explains what will happen to those that reject him.

> 42 Jesus said to them, "Have you never read in the Scriptures:
>
> "'The stone that the builders rejected has become the cornerstone; this was the Lord's doing, and it is marvelous in our eyes'?
>
> 43 Therefore I tell you, the kingdom of God will be taken away from you and given to a people producing its fruits. 44 And the one who falls on this stone will be broken to pieces; and when it falls on anyone, it will crush him." (Matthew 21:42-44)

Many may hear the Gospel and it goads them into rejecting its message. For this person the option chosen is that of surrender. They have to be made to give in. The Gospel will feel like a battle to be won, and yet they will never overcome. The Bible says that every knee will bow (Philippians 2:10-11). The sad reality is that this bowing will happen when it is too late for it make a difference.

Unlike those that will be forced to acknowledge the goodness of the Good News, there are those that hear the gospel and rejoice because it truly is Good News to their hearts.

14 But thank God! He has made us his captives and continues to lead us along in Christ's triumphal procession. Now he uses us to spread the knowledge of Christ everywhere, like a sweet perfume. 15 Our lives are a Christ-like fragrance rising up to God. But this fragrance is perceived differently by those who are being saved and by those who are perishing. 16 To those who are perishing, we are a dreadful smell of death and doom. But to those who are being saved, we are a life-giving perfume. (2 Corinthians 2:14-16a, NLT)

Submit yourself unto the Lord and allow God to order your steps.

OBEDIENCE IS GREATER THAN SACRIFICE

Jesus' final admonition to the disciples has been called the Great Commission. Matthew records it this way for us at the end of his Gospel:

> [19] "Therefore go and make disciples of all nations, baptizing them in the name of the Father and of the Son and of the Holy Spirit, [20] and teaching them to obey everything I have commanded you. And surely I am with you always, to the very end of the age." (Matthew 28:19-20, NIV)

Jesus said in another place, "And you are my friends, if you obey me" (John 15:14

CEV). The idea in the word "obey" is that of a continuing process. Jesus is telling us we are His friends and His faithful servants if "we keep on doing" what He commands. Too often, we have separated our belief in Jesus with our obedience to Jesus. John tells us that to do this is to actually say that we are liars and that the truth we claim is not really in us (1 John 2:4). I have often wondered at the meaning of this phrase: Obedience is Greater than Sacrifice. Only recently have I begun understand its meaning.

When God makes His will known, we are commanded to obey. But what if the result of obedience is death, as it was for Jesus? What will we do then? I think that this is the mystery inherent in the command. God is not asking us to submit to pain, suffering or injustice. God has called us to submit to Him, trusting that the ends that lie outside of our sight will not only achieve the ultimate will and purposes of God, but will bring to us our greatest satisfaction. We must never forget that we died when we accepted, in faith, the life of Christ as our own (Galatians 2:20).

Sacrifice can be self-serving because it can validate us and our motives. But obedience only serves the greater good of the one who commanded us to act. When we obey we are bending our will to that of our King. If we have committed our lives to the service of Jesus, then everything else is just what we do in the line of duty. No more reward will be offered other than the praise of our God, "Well done, good and faithful servant" (Matthew 25:21). Is that enough for you? (cf. Matthew 8:1-13) Listen to the parable that Jesus gave about the wrong attitude of a servant of God.

> 7"Will any one of you who has a servant plowing or keeping sheep say to him when he has come in from the field, 'Come at once and recline at table'? 8 Will he not rather say to him, 'Prepare supper for me, and dress properly, and serve me while I eat and drink, and afterward you will eat and drink'? 9 Does he thank the servant because he did what was commanded? 10 So you also, when you have done all that you were commanded, say, 'We are unworthy servants; we have only done what was our duty.' " (Luke 17:7-10)

"We have only done what was our duty." When we have given our all in serving Jesus, we have only just begun.

THE DEATH OF DEATH

One of the most glorious realities of the Christian faith is that death has been defeated. The crucifixion and death of Jesus, God demonstrates the fullness of His love. The sacrificial system of the old covenant is replaced by the sacrificial death of God, in the person of Jesus, for me (Hebrews 9:11-28, 10:11-14)! (I think too often we don't personalize the salvation that Jesus purchased for all people in a way that makes it meaningful.) When we add this remarkable truth to the equally wonderful truth that Jesus was raised from the dead we are confronted with a new reality—Death's power has been destroyed, not just for now, but forever!

Paul tells us that it was through Sin that death was introduced into the world (Romans 5:12). It is because of this Sin that death brings fear to our hearts and minds and we find our joy melting away. Paul again tells us in Romans 6:23a that "the wages of sin is death." We have earned the death that we will have to suffer, both in its physical and spiritual effects, because of our tendency to follow after our own will rather than God's. We have earned the penalty of sin, but God has done something so incomprehensible that most who hear this message don't believe it (cf. 1 Corinthians 1:18-31).

Even though we have earned death, "the free gift of God is eternal life in Christ Jesus our Lord" (Romans 6:23b). Because Jesus took upon himself the punishment for Sin which He had not committed, Jesus was able to deflect the justified wrath of God away from us and absorbed that wrath upon Himself. This is called the doctrine of Propitiation (cf. Romans 3:25; Hebrews 2:17; 1 John 2:2, 4:10). The more I study this word the more amazed I am at what God did in order to make salvation a possibility for sinners.

Even with this reality we still must pass through the dark door of physical death. In the death of Jesus Christ on the cross, death is defeated and we no longer have to fear what is waiting on the "other side." If we follow Jesus He will lead us through death into new life–a life purchased with His own death and resurrection. Jesus told the disciples that he was going to prepare the way and the place.

1 "Don't let your hearts be troubled. Trust in God, and trust also in me. 2 There is more than enough room in my Father's home. If this were not so, would I have told you that I am going to prepare a place for you? 3 When everything is ready, I will come and get you, so that you will always be with me where I am. 4 And you know the way to where I am going."

5 "No, we don't know, Lord," Thomas said. "We have no idea where you are going, so how can we know the way?"

6 Jesus told him, "I am the way, the truth, and the life. No one can come to the Father except through me. 7 If you had really known me, you would know who my Father is. From now on, you do know him and have seen him!" (John 14:1-7, NLT)

The way is Jesus. To know Jesus is to know how to get to the Father's house. To know Jesus is to see God. The challenge then is to remember what we have come to know and to live accordingly.

VICTORY!

My hope and prayer is that you have benefitted from the time spent looking at the multi-faceted diamond of the Gospel. We have discovered that God is holy and that our sin has kept us separated from God. We have looked to Jesus as the ultimate remedy for reconciliation with God. We have been confronted with the fact that it is through repentance that salvation is applied to us. As a result of salvation, we are given a new life, a new purpose and a new journey.

The Gospel is such a wonderful truth if we would just embrace it and live it out to the end. The Gospel is not complex, but it is complete. The Gospel is not easy, but it is simple. If we strive to know, understand and live according to everything that it contains we will live a life that is a joy to us and pleasing to our Father in Heaven.

One of the most comforting realities of the Christian faith is that we are provided with the final scene. God inspires hope in His children because He is able to let us take a peek at what awaits us. Paul, in First Corinthians, provides us with some insight into what he calls a mystery. A mystery is not something that is unknowable, but rather something that has not yet been made known. Paul declares a mystery for all that believe in Jesus Christ:

> 51 "Behold! I tell you a mystery. ... 54 When the perishable puts on the imperishable, and the mortal puts on immortality, then shall come to pass the saying that is written: 'Death is swallowed up in victory.' 55 'O death, where is your victory? O death, where is your sting?' 56 The sting of death is sin, and the power of sin is the law. 57 But thanks be to God, who gives us the victory through our Lord Jesus Christ (1 Corinthians 15:51, 54–57)

I believe the Gospel's ultimate power lies in its ability to bring Victory over sin; Victory over Death; Victory over hell; Victory over Satan ; and finally Victory over self and selfishness. Victory ought to be the way of life for the Christian. I do not mean that we will not face trials and difficult times because we will (James 1:2-4; 1 Peter 4:12-14, 16). We should

Victory!

expect these as a natural part of the Christian journey and experience. However, in spite of these we will remember what God has done. We will remember the Joy of the Gospel and rejoice continually for the good thing God has done for us, in us and will do through us in the world.

We have Victory in Christ! Learn to love the Gospel and live according to its truth "for it is the power of God unto salvation for all who will believe it" (Romans 1:16).

WHICH ARE YOU?

Have you experienced the Joy of the Gospel? This is where we began our journey. This is the ultimate gift of our gracious heavenly Father to those who have been adopted. If you have never believed in Jesus and accepted the gift of of His death and Resurrection as payment for your Sin why not do it today?

Or do you need to Re-joy in the Gospel? Maybe you are a Christian and have lost sight of what God has given you in the Gospel. Do you need to ask God to return to you the joy of your salvation just like King David did (Psalm 51:12)?

Gospel BASICS

Which ever place you find yourself, God is calling you to come back. Repentance is the act of turning away from anything and everything that would distract you from God.

Let me be honest with you, this can be a slow and grueling process, but as we continue to walk with God and call upon God, He promises to send the Holy Spirit to help us (John 16:7). If we are going to live according to the will of God, we must learn to trust and obey the commandments of God. A good place to start is to read Colossians. This short letter helps us see what God's priorities are and how the the expectations of the world are not the same as those God has for us who claim to be Christians. I have included a reading plan as an appendix that will help you grow in your dependence upon God, who is our heavenly Father.

If you have never turned your life over to God I would encourage you to look at "The Way of Salvation" in the appendix. As you go through each step, open your heart and mind and ask God the Father to speak to you about who He wants you to become.

You're almost done. On the following page, space has been provided for you to write down what you have learned in this study. Answer the question that started it all: "What is the Gospel?" When you are done go back to page "x" and compare.

We have reached the end of our study and exploration of the Gospel. The gospel is the most important message that has ever been proclaimed. What makes it important is not that it has been written about, preached or taught by thousands and millions of men and women throughout human history. What makes the Gospel important is that it is the message proclaimed by God Himself.

What is the Gospel?

_____

_____

_____

_____

_____

_____

_____

_____

_____

_____

_____

_____

_____

_____

_____

_____

_____

APPENDIXES

CONTEXTUALIZED READING PLAN

This reading pattern is what I use when I disciple new and growing Christians. I call this reading plan "**Contextualized Reading**." Reading large portions of Scripture has proven helpful in discerning God's thoughts in the text that is read. The Goal is 25-30 chapters a week. **So read everyday!**

There are three bookmarks that I give out that are outlined below. You should consider writing this plan in your bible to make it easier to recall the progression. These bookmarks do not cover the entire bible. My hope is that after the first three you will continue using the pattern that you have learned and complete the reading of the bible on your own, and as you are led to disciple someone else you will begin again reading with those that you disciple.

Each number is a week. Week one, read Colossians 7 times. Week two, read 1 John 6 times and so on. Read everyday and you will hear God speak!

Bookmark 1

1. Colossians (7x's)
2. 1 John (6x's)
3. Ephesians (5x's)
4. Galatians (5x's)
5. 1 Peter (6x's)
6. Philemon & Jude (7x's)
7. Philippians (6x's)
8. James (5x's)
9. 1 Corinthians (2x's)

Bookmark 2

1. Jonah (7x's)
2. Esther (3x's)
3. 2 Timothy (7x's)
4. Proverbs (1x)
5. Judges (1x)
6. Titus (7x's)

7. Nehemiah (2x's)
8. Mark (1x)
9. John (1x)
10. 2 Peter (2x's)
11. 1 Thessalonians (6x's)
12. 1 Timothy (5x's)
13. Acts (1x)

Bookmark 3

1. Joshua (1x)
2. Hebrews (2x's)
3. Haggai (7x's)
4. 2 Corinthians (2x's)
5. 2 Thessalonians (7x's)
6. Malachi (6x's)
7. Ezra (3x's)
8. Matthew (1x)
9. Amos (3x)
10. Hosea (2x's)
11. Romans (2x's)
12. Luke 1-12 (2x's)
13. Luke 13-24 (2x's)
14. Ruth (7x's)

THE WAY OF
SALVATION

(Take the time to look up the scriptures that go with each step. This is not a formula. Allow the word of God to work its power in you. The prayers are provided as a guide, but can be prayed as your own.)

❖ Acknowledge that there is a God and that God is Holy.
   ❑ Psalm 53:1
   ❑ Hebrews 11:6

Prayer: Father, I have not always acknowledged you as God in my life. Help me to submit my desire to rule my life over to you. Amen.

❖ Recognize that Sin does exist in the world.
   ❑Psalm 106:6-8
   ❑Romans 5:12

Prayer: Father, I don't have to look far to know that there is something wrong with this world. I cannot pretend to escape the influence of Sin. Help me to know that this is not what you desire for me. Open my heart to accept your way and live by it. Amen.

❖ Admit that Sin is not just "out there," but that it is in your heart as well.

❑ Genesis 6:5

❑ Ezekiel 36:26-28

Prayer: Father, I have acknowledged your presence in my life and the presence of sin in the world, but I need to confess that sin is also present in me. Father, help me to mourn my sin and to not enjoy its deceptive fruit. Amen.

❖ Repent of your participation in the system of the world. Commit to turning away from anything and everything that is not of God in your life.

❑ Psalm 7:12-17

❑ 2 Chronicles 7:14

❑ Ephesians 2:1-7

❑ Galatians 5:16-24

❑ 1 Peter 4:2

❑ 1 John 3:7

Prayer: Father, I desire to repent from my Sin. I no longer desire to practice any behavior that is contrary to your standard of living. Give me strength, O God, to turn and face you. Amen.

❖ Agree with God that you have failed to meet God's standard of living.
- ☐ Romans 3:23
- ☐ Isaiah 64:6

Prayer: Lord, I have failed to meet your standard, but you have re-created me. I have repented and you have forgiven my Sin because of Jesus. I have new life and I ask that you would work in me a new way of living. Amen.

❖ Look to Jesus as the remedy to the Sin in your life and believe, trust that Jesus is able and has the power to remove the stain of sin from your life.
- ☐ Romans 10:9, 13
- ☐ John 10:9
- ☐ Acts 16:31

Prayer: Father, I know that I can't reach you on my own. I believe that you sent Jesus to stand in my place of Judgment and I thank you for your grace. I accept the righteousness of Christ as my own and will no longer accept the condemnation of my forgiven past, present and future! Amen.

❖ Begin to Obey the Commandments of God as written in the Word

❑ 1 John (entire letter)

Prayer: Father, enable me to obey your commandments, not as chore or a burden, but as the expression of gratitude for the grace and love you have given to me. Amen.

ABOUT THE AUTHOR

Victor R. Scott met his wife in high school and they have been happily married since 2003. They have two daughters born four years apart, on the same day.

He is the eldest of four. His father is a retired army chaplain and his mother is a retired Special Education teacher's assistant. They serve as the lead pastors of *Ambassadors of Christ Fellowship* church in Columbus, Georgia.

Victor is a graduate of Georgia Southern University earning a *Bachelor of Arts* (2002) in Sociology with a minor in Philosophy. He completed his *Master of Divinity* degree from Luther Rice University and Seminary (2011) in Lithonia, Georgia.

He currently serves as the *Director of Youth Ministries* and *Assistant to the Pastor* at the First United Methodist Church in Cordele, Georgia, where he is active in one-on-one discipleship with youth, adults, and pastors using the "Contextualized Reading" method described in the appendix. He is also an occasional blogger and growing twitter user.

Proof

Made in the USA
Charleston, SC
25 June 2011